WALKS AROUND Hawes

10 WALKS UNDER 6 MILES

Dalesman

Dalesman Publishing Company Ltd
Stable Courtyard, Broughton Hall,
Skipton, North Yorkshire BD23 3AZ

First Edition 1999

Text © Richard Musgrave

Illustrations © Christine Isherwood:
p5 Gayle Beck, p8 Appersett viaduct, p15 greater bellflower,
p17 ring ouzel, p19 large heath cotton grass, p24 yew, p28 redstart,
p32 common sandpiper

Maps by Jeremy Ashcroft

Cover : Gayle Beck by Colin Raw

A British Library Cataloguing in Publication record
is available for this book

ISBN 85568 158 7

Printed by Amadeus Press, Huddersfield

Contents

Introduction

The western end of Wensleydale is encircled by a range of high, undulating fells. A terrestrial paradise? Particularly so for those able to escape from the main tourist zones, on foot. Far from the madding crowds, indeed!

There's a lot to see in and around Hawes. Attractions include a fine folk museum and the Wensleydale creamery and cheese visitor centre. There are also lots of neighbouring villages and many of these are visited during the walks included in this book. Places like Hardraw where England's highest single drop waterfall is found. Simonstone, Sedbusk, Bainbridge, Worton and Askrigg – a village renowned for its clockmaking industry during the 17th and 18th centuries. More recently the associations with the television programme *All Creatures Great and Small*.

Also visited are the Norse 'shielings' or settlements, villages with names ending sett. Appersett, Burtersett, Countersett and Marsett.

All these together with wildflower sprinkled meadows, some containing paved paths, waterfalls, a Roman Road and a "haunted" lake, make for a perfect series of outings on foot. The walks included aren't too demanding and should be within the capabilities of reasonably fit persons.

United Bus Company run services to most of the locations from Hawes excepting the Semerwater area (Walks 9 and 10). For service details contact local Tourist Information Centres or telephone 01325 468771.

In 1998 The Wensleydale Railway Association began a regular bus service in Wensleydale connecting with the Settle to Carlisle railway. For details contact Hawes TIC on 01969 667450

To complement this book it would be useful to have OS Outdoor Leisure Map 30, or Stile Publication maps Hawes and District and possibly the Aysgarth area as well.

My sincerest hope is that you'll enjoy the walks.

J. Richard Musgrave
January 1999

Aysgill Force

Length of walk: 3 miles
Start: Main car park, Hawes
Terrain: Easy

The village of Gayle and the little town of Hawes lie side by side but are worlds apart in many ways. One thing that they do have in common is cheese — for the famous Hawes Creamery is situated between the two.

This walk visits Aysgill Force and the shallow, stepped ledges which form the spectacular falls close to Gayle Bridge.

Set off from the car park opposite The Board Hotel turning right to walk along the main street in Hawes. Bear right at the Midland Bank to swing

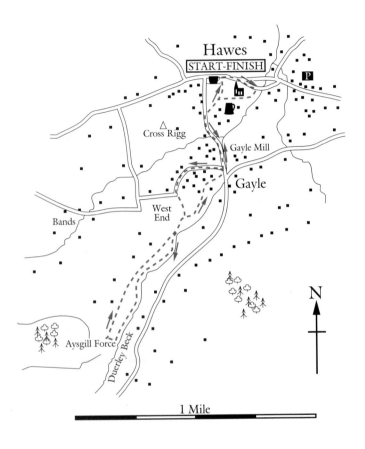

right again opposite the White Hart Inn to enter a cobbled path which leads around the church to a stile.

Follow a paved meadow path to emerge at a main road. Turn left towards Gayle and walk along the road to a junction, turning right, immediately beyond Gayle Laithe. Follow the narrow lane, passing the Rookhurst Hotel and negotiate a double bend, to arrive at a junction. Veer right to a stile signposted Pennine Way and continue across the fields to another Pennine Way sign.

At this point ignore the Pennine Way route; instead veer left to another stile across the field to descend some steps and follow the riverside path to Aysgill Falls — a 40ft waterfall in Duerley Beck.

Continue beyond the waterfall for a short distance, walking alongside the beck. After crossing a stile swing right, leaving the beck side (if you reach a footbridge across Duerley Beck, you've missed the turning point) to climb the steep field to a ladder stile. Beyond the ladder stile you can play gap stile spotting, as a succession of stiles leads across the meadows returning to a stile used on the outward leg, marked with a yellow indicator. Wether Fell is away on the right.

From this stile walk straight on with Hawes church directly ahead. On reaching another stile ignore the Pennine Way route (used earlier); instead continue straight on to another stile and the road and turn right.

Walk along the narrow streets of Gayle to arrive at the road bridge and a view of the waterfalls. Don't cross the bridge; instead turn left to follow the road which is signposted – Hawes.

Follow the road just beyond Wensleydale Creamery, then pass through a gated stile and return to the car park.

Appersett Viaduct

Length of walk: 3 miles
Start from: Hawes
Terrain: Mainly fields

The feature of this outing is the five arch viaduct near Appersett, formerly part of the Wensleydale Railway. Widdale Beck tumbles from the surrounding fells, passing beneath the viaduct in spectacular style.

Leave the car park opposite The Board Hotel in Hawes, via the corner gap stile which leads up through the main car park and across a field towards the Wensleydale Cheese Visitor Centre. Leave the field by the gate stile, cross the road and follow the signpost to Mossy Lane/Youth Hostel, swinging left at a barn to walk uphill to another barn.

Walking in a straight line pass through a succession of stiles to cross Mossy Lane, continuing to a roofless barn before swinging right and emerging on a road. Turn left along the road for 30 yards to a gate signposted Thorney Mire House.

A clear path leads between two walls, curving left at a wall angle; then continues a good distance across

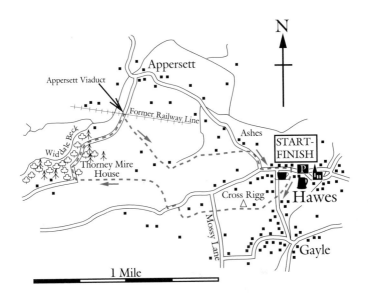

rough pasture towards a gate. Pass through the gate, turning right along the road beyond Thorney Mire House, to arrive at Appersett viaduct. At this point swing right to pass through the gate following the route to Ashes (name of a farm near Hawes). **There is no right of way along the former railway**.

From the gate head diagonally right, seeking a narrow stile in the facing wall, then continue uphill along a clear path. Reaching the crown of the hill the route unfurls beyond a gate, across a field towards a ladder stile set alongside a barn near the trees. Wether Fell makes a spectacular backdrop.

From this ladder stile, cross the field in an easterly direction towards a gap stile beneath a large tree. Maintain the same course, and with the wall to your right negotiate another stile close to a clump of trees. Pass through a gate and continue directly onwards to the main road. Turn right and return to Hawes. Notice the milking scene inscribed high on the school wall, indicative of Hawes' long associations with dairy farming.

Sedbusk and Simonstone – Hardraw Force

Length of walk: 4 or 5 miles
Start: Hawes
Terrain: Short uphill section to Sedbusk.
Remainder easy going

Another outing starting from the busy market town of Hawes. This crosses Wensleydale's river — the Ure — to visit three small settlements. Sedbusk, Simonstone and Hardraw. Additionally, as in Walk 4, the opportunity to extend the walk by a mile and to visit England's highest single drop waterfall, Hardraw Force, is presented.

Walk eastwards along the main street, turning left at the Midland Bank. Continue downhill, turning left at a junction towards Hardraw. After crossing the road bridge over the Ure look for a stile/signpost on the right to Sedbusk.

A clear path leads over a tiny, cobbled bridge to a gated stile, then crosses the field towards some trees. Cross the road, enter the field opposite following the indicator towards Sedbusk Lane.

The path crosses two intervening stiles to arrive at Sedbusk Lane. Turn right, then after half a dozen paces pass through the stile on the left — signposted

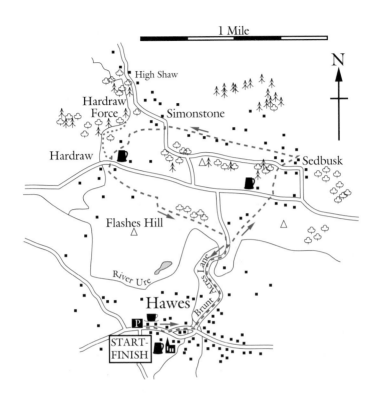

Simonstone. Head diagonally left to another stile, then set off across the meadows maintaining a straight line for an enjoyable mile towards Simonstone. Staggs Fell overlooks on the right.

Leave the fields soon after passing some farm buildings by a stile situated to the left of a gate. Turn left to walk on the road for a few paces before turning right — signposted Hardraw.

Continue with some cottages on the right seeking a stile on the left before arriving at Simonstone Hall, a hotel, and formerly a hunting lodge belonging to the Earl of Wharncliffe, a local benefactor of the time.

After passing through the stile note the dozens of empty gin bottles in the gardens of the Hall. These were unearthed about a decade ago and it's thought they were emptied by a previous incumbent!

Pass through a second stile, then head across the field towards the farm buildings. Some fine walking sticks for sale when I passed by. Beyond the farm swing left to descend along a clear path to enter the hamlet of Hardraw. The option of the waterfall visit is available through the bar of the Green Dragon — there's a charge. Either way cross the road, seeking a stile to the right of the Shepherd's Kitchen — signposted Brunt Acres Road.

Veer left, then count the stiles. After passing the fifth, veer right towards a stone, step stile set in the wall, turning left to walk alongside a row of trees and an exposed limestone scar. The path briefly touches the river before heading across the field towards a gate alongside some trees.

Turn right along the road for the return into Hawes.

A section of the Pennine Way and Hardraw Force

Length of walk: 4 or 5 miles
Start: Appersett
Terrain: Mainly meadows and a riverside stroll.
Brief uphill section to reach Pennine Way
Bus Service: Wensleydale Tourer. Circular route
Details 0891 910910

Appersett is situated on the A684, just over a mile north west of Hawes. Apart from the through traffic it's a quiet place, housing a farming community and a haulage family. Widdale Beck tumbles from the higher reaches, passing through the village to amalgamate with the Ure 400 yards downstream.

Set out from the car parking area opposite Bridge End cottage. Cross the road bridge (Appersett Bridge) then to alleviate road walking use the ladder stile (Mossdale Head) and walk the short distance to another road bridge (New Bridge). Cross the bridge, swinging left towards a junction. At the junction turn right and pass through a stile signposted Bluebell Hill.

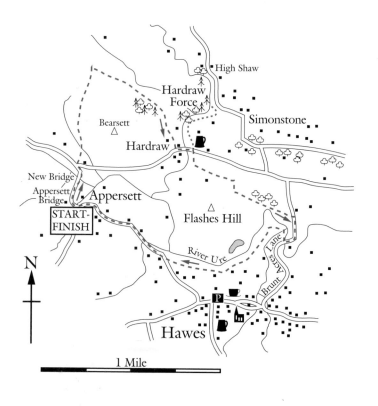

Proceed across the field, pass through a gate, and then veer left, uphill towards another gate. A clear path leads across an open pasture with several waymarkers to aid navigation. The big hills of Wensleydale are evident at this point.

Make towards a ladder stile directly ahead, situated 50 yards to the right of a plantation. From the ladder stile maintain the same line, alongside the wall, to emerge into an enclosed lane and turn right. This is the Pennine Way route, and it is followed to Hardraw.

Eventually the lane descends, and the rooftops of Hardraw and the church come into view. Across the valley Hawes is evident, with Wether Fell an impressive backdrop.

Swing left into Hardraw, and those wanting to take in Hardraw Force (England's highest single drop waterfall) can do so by passing through the bar of the Green Dragon. There is a charge. Otherwise, after crossing the road bridge turn right, cross a stile (signposted Brunt Acres Road) then veer left to walk along a paved path.

Walk in a straight line across a succession of fields, each linked by stiles, to arrive at Brunt Acres Road and turn right. Follow the road across the road bridge then enter the field on the right — signposted Appersett. Cross the footbridge, head towards a telegraph pole, then walk diagonally left towards an iron ladder stile.

A wondrous mile alongside the Ure ensues, before emerging onto a road just beyond a sign stating 'Fishing Access' only. Turn right and follow the road into Appersett.

Mill Gill and the Waterfalls

Length of walk: 3 miles (Excluding Whitfield Gill Force)
Start: Askrigg
Terrain: Uphill outward. Downhill return
Bus Service: 156 and 157 from Hawes

Any visit to the Hawes area should include a detour to Askrigg. Those who remember the television series *All Creatures Great and Small* will surely be aware that Askrigg became the fictitious Darrowby during the 70s and 80s.

Mill Gill contains several spectacular waterfalls, including Whitfield Gill Force, which is located at the furthest point of the right of way. To reach this waterfall one has to endure a tortuous 400 yards along an unpleasant, well-used, muddy, uneven route. Whitfield Gill Force is an optional extra to the walk set out.

Pass to the right side of St Oswald's church. Follow the lane, seeking a stile 100 yards beyond the last house — signposted Mill Gill Force.

Make towards the mill buildings, passing beneath the aqueduct, before crossing a footbridge and turning right. The flat-topped Addleborough will be obvious, at this stage.

The route, which is well waymarked, meanders through a bluebell wonderland (in season), and on reaching an obvious junction, veer right to take in Mill Gill Force. The walk continues following the other fork to arrive at a gated stile close to a footbridge. Swing left here signposted Whitfield Gill (ignore the footbridge).

The option to visit Whitfield Gill Force arrives soon afterwards, at a pronounced junction. The walk route veers right (Low Straits Lane), descending to cross a footbridge after which you turn right. Follow the clear path as it rises and curves left all the way to Low Straits Lane. In the winter months Whitfield Gill Force will be visible through the bare trees as the ascent to Low Straits Lane nears conclusion.

Turn right along Low Straits Lane, with wonderful views rapidly appearing. Bainbridge and Askrigg are seen, in that order.

The clue to the departure from the lane is a tiny barn on the left. Just beyond this and prior to reaching a ford, turn right through a wide gate and enter a field. Walk past a barn, continuing in the same line to pass through a narrow, gap stile. Pass to the left of another barn, aiming towards a gated stile 15 yards to the right of a wide gate. A ruined barn is a useful indicator.

Pass through this and the adjacent stile, swinging left across the field to pass through an open gateway. With the roofs of Askrigg in sight, pass to the right of another ruined barn (fine archway) seeking a gated stile hiding in the right hand corner of the field.

Nearing the conclusion of the walk, proceed in a straight line with the wall on the right towards a small, Victorian, wrought iron gate. Pass through to emerge on the main street in Askrigg. Turn right to the church.

Nappa Hall and Newbiggin

Length of walk: 4 miles
Start: Askrigg Church
Terrain: Mainly fields. Lots of stiles
Bus Service: 156 and 157 from Hawes

Follow the main road downhill beyond the church and The Temperance Hall, turning left into a lane running alongside the animal feeds factory. This leads directly to the River Ure, but 20 yards before reaching the river, swing left making towards a signpost. The way soon resumes a riverside setting, continuing downstream to Worton Bridge.

While enjoying the riverside scenery a glimpse left reveals Askrigg, nestling beneath Ellerkin Scar, and the road to Swaledale wriggling over the horizon. Closer to Worton Bridge the castellated outline of Nappa Hall will be seen.

Emerging from the fields at the bridge turn left seeking a stile on the right – signposted Aysgarth. Continue along the riverbank, then cross

19

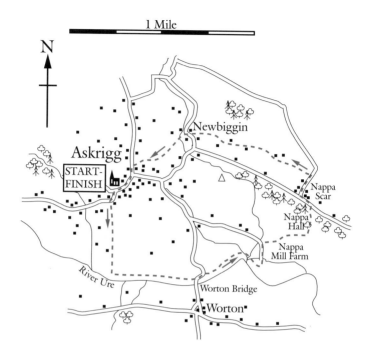

a footbridge and head towards Nappa Mill Farm (Nappa House).

At the farm swing left, walking away from the buildings along the access road. Don't cross the bridge; instead hop over the stile making diagonally across the field towards a gate in the far corner, near a telegraph pole.

Maintain the previous line over the next field to arrive at a lane, then turn left to walk past Nappa Hall emerging on a main road. Note the milk churns on the wall!

Nappa Hall was originally built as a fortified manor house, at the time of the Scottish raids, for the powerful Metcalfe family. In recent times it has functioned as a working farm and bed and breakfast accommodation.

Turn left along the main road, turning right at the first opportunity, to enter a small hamlet. Seek a stile beyond the last building on the left signposted Newbiggin. Walking in an almost straight line cross a dozen fields, to arrive at another tiny hamlet — Newbiggin. Along the way look across the valley for the unmistakable straight line of the Roman Road, snaking over Wether Fell.

At Newbiggin walk around the small 'green' to enter a lane alongside a large barn. After a few paces pass through a gated stile on the left, then follow a well-used path across the field towards a wall angle. Maintain the same line, passing through another stile, pass a bath, with the rooftops of Askrigg in view.

The exit stile is hidden by trees close to some cottages but is easily located. At the road swing left, returning to Askrigg.

Brough Scar and Worton

> **Length of walk: 4 miles**
> **Start: Bainbridge**
> **Terrain: Easy: One brief uphill section**

Bainbridge is a spacious location built around a large green area. There's a pub, a post office and a garage that sells everything. Lots of roadside parking and a bus service from Hawes. Numbers 156 and 157 serve the village.

Long ago the village was a Roman garrison town, known then as Virosidium. Little remains of the Roman presence except the Roman Road, which travels over Wether Fell and on to Ribchester in Lancashire 30 plus miles away. Walk 9 treads a section of that road.

England's shortest river, the Bain, just two miles long, runs along the eastern edge of the village.

Leave the village at the opposite end to the public house. Cross the road bridge — Bain bridge— noting the splendid waterfalls. Continue beyond the garage to the junction for Semerwater. At that point veer right and locate a stile signposted Cubeck.

An uphill section commences, making diagonally towards the small cluster of trees on the hilltop. Superb views of Bainbridge, Askrigg and the surrounding countryside are presented from this lofty position. The exposed limestone ridge is known as Brough Scar.

Pass through the stile and swing left, commencing a level and straight route along the scar top. The path is clear and eventually enters a wooded area. Seek a signpost to Worton and descend through the woodland to a stile (lots of wild garlic hereabouts in season).

Follow the indication of the signpost towards a wall end, continuing diagonally across the field towards the exit gate alongside the farm buildings.

Cross over the A684 road to enter the hamlet of Worton noting the inscription on the gable end of the first house. The said Michael Smith not only built the house, but he quarried and carted the stone used. The house dates from 1729.

Within the hamlet swing left at the junction, descending to the road bridge.

Cross the bridge and veer left through a stile signposted Askrigg. An obvious path rolls out across the meadows, crossing the disused railway and into Askrigg.

Enter the churchyard, passing to the left of the church. Walk beyond the porch; pass in front of some cottages then, after crossing a field, arrive at the main road.

At the road turn right, continuing beyond Low Mill Outdoor Centre and a school. Immediately beyond the school, cross the road to enter a lane (signpost). Hop over a stile and swing right.

Walk alongside the former Wensleydale railway, eventually passing to the right hand side of a house and cross a footbridge. Veer left towards Yore Bridge and turn left for a quick return into Bainbridge.

The High Path to Gayle

Length of walk: 3 miles
Start: Burtersett
Terrain: Easy. Lots of stiles

Burtersett nestles beneath a high point named Yorburgh, and has attracted the attentions of the paragliding fraternity in recent times. Those who engage themselves in those activities will undoubtedly achieve spectacular views of upper Wensleydale.

If you prefer to keep both feet on the ground — and still obtain views from an elevated position, this is the walk for you. Roadside car parking at the top end of the village.

Start from the top end of the village, leaving Burtersett in a westerly direction. There's a signpost to Gayle. Enter an uneven lane — Shaws Lane — with wonderful views of Wensleydale. Yorburgh (515m) presides high on the left. Hawes church will be visible towards the lane end.

Leaving the enclosed section behind, pass between some barns heading towards a gated stile, then maintaining the same line cross four additional stiles to arrive at a fork in the path close to a barn.

At this point veer left — signposted Gayle south — and cross a ladder stile 50 yards beyond the barn. A succession of stiles leads across the meadows. Confirmation that you're treading the correct route can be made by noting a series of barns 30 yards to the left.

Ten paces prior to reaching a wide metal gate, swing right passing through a tiny gated stile to follow a clear path towards a road. Turn right, along the road, descending to Gayle alongside the spectacular waterfalls.

Don't cross the bridge, instead swing right, following the Bainbridge road. There are some attractive buildings at Gayle. Local pride is obvious.

Soon after passing Blackburn House farm, pass through a stile on the right signposted Burtersett. The path leads towards a campsite with Wether Fell and Yorburgh prominent, on the right. Staggs Fell rests on the opposite side of the valley.

Pass in front of the farmhouse seeking a stile in the wall facing, then continue across the meadows crossing a further six stiles, before swinging right and rising upwards towards the village. Enter the village close to a building painted white. Turn right; pass the former Wesleyan Chapel to return to your car.

*Paved meadow paths are common in Wensleydale. Usually these led to a church, and ensured footwear and the hems of crinolines were kept clean.

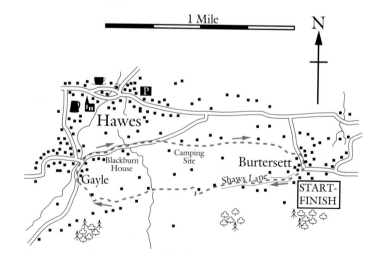

The River Bain and the Roman Road

Length of walk: 5¹/₂ miles
Start: Countersett or Semerwater Bridge
Terrain: The hardest walk in the book!

Countersett is known mainly for associations with the Quaker faith. Countersett Hall, the large white gabled building and a private residence, was formerly the home of Richard Robinson — the first Quaker in Wensleydale. George Fox, the founder of the movement, visited the hall in 1677. Robinson died in 1693 and is buried in the Quaker burial ground at Bainbridge.

Worthy of a visit is the recently refurbished Friends' Meeting House at Countersett. This is located 30 yards beyond the telephone box. If parking at the roadside at Countersett, please park tidily.

Whichever location you elect to start from pass through the stile close to Semerwater Bridge — signposted Bainbridge. Follow England's shortest river, The Bain (two miles long), for approximately one mile to arrive at a ladder stile. At that point the river curves left and is forsaken in favour of a green, uphill, swathe.

Cross three stiles in quick succession, then make for the round topped summit of Bracken Hill, aiming to the left of the plateau. Reaching the highest point look back to admire the scene. A brief descent leads to a gated stile and onwards towards a large sheepfold.

Keep to the topside (right) of this, veering slightly left, eventually walking with a wall on the right. Bainbridge will be evident directly ahead. A stile leads onto a road and is followed into Bainbridge, passing a garage, which sells almost everything.

Cross the road bridge (Bainbridge!), then swing first left, noting the old Dame School building which was founded by Mrs Eliza Blades sometime in the 1860s. At Beech House veer right then proceed as indicated through a wide gate, and along a house driveway to a stile/gate.

A clear path passes to the left of a large barn, then leads uphill across several fields emerging at a stile situated to the right of a farmhouse (Gill Edge). Turn right along the access road, and right again at the junction. Walk down the road for 400 yards then swing left to enter a wide, uneven lane. This is the route of the Roman Road, which originally travelled the 30 miles between Bainbridge (Virosidium) and Ribchester in Lancashire.

This historical route is followed for about a mile, until a narrow stile (which isn't obvious) is located on the left. The precise location of the stile is identified being 100 yards before the uneven lane crosses a proper road.

From the stile follow a faint path, upwards, through the tufted grass keeping adjacent to the wall on the right. Eventually the path becomes clearer, leading ever closer to the wall and a stile. This location is known as Hawes End.

Turn left along the road for 100 yards to pass through a gate signposted Countersett.

The descent to Countersett presents wonderful vistas, particularly so on reaching the second stile. Beyond this

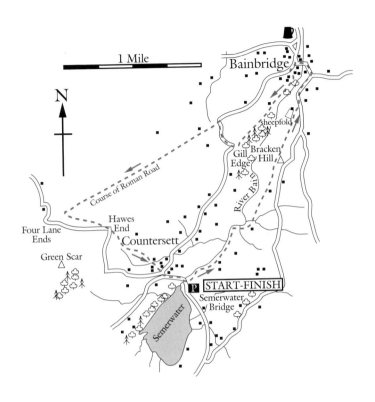

veer diagonally left, seeking a stile in the wall situated in a line between the water purification equipment and a barn.

Pass the barn maintaining a downward course for 20 yards — then veer right towards the trees to locate a stile hidden in the depression. Don't descend as far as the second barn.

From the stile cross the field towards a gate situated to the right of the houses. Maintain the previous line to the end of the track and turn right then left to Semerwater Bridge. If wanting to visit the Friends' Meeting House turn left for 100 yards.

A circuit of Semerwater

> **Length of walk: 4 miles**
> **Start: Semerwater Bridge**
> **Terrain: Easy throughout**

Legend tells of a village resting beneath the serene Semerwater, although no evidence has ever corroborated this. This expanse of water, and Malham Tarn further south, are the only 'lakes' within the Yorkshire Dales National Park.

From the Countersett side of Semerwater Bridge pass through a gate — signposted Marsett Lane. Follow the waymarks to arrive at the lane, then turn left to follow the road all the way to Marsett. It's a quiet road and the scenery is wonderful, so enjoy yourselves despite the unavoidable road work. Along the way note the miniature "castle" gateposts at Wood End.

At Marsett cross the bridge then swing left. There is a signpost (amid the collection of redundant farm implements), to Semerwater and Stalling Busk. Briefly accompany the beck, before passing through a gate and head towards a footbridge. Stalling Busk will be in sight, halfway up the facing hillside.

Cross the footbridge, swinging left to cross some marshy ground to another footbridge (if it's really wet go further left). Again cross the bridge and veer left to pass through a stile in the wall to your right. Head directly towards a barn, turning left through a stile. (If you want to visit Stalling Busk turn right at this point towards Busk Lane, then turn left up the hill.)

Follow a well-trodden path, passing a succession of stiles to arrive at the site of the ruined lakeside church built in 1722 to replace an earlier construction erected in 1603. Pass to the right of the church (the grounds are open to the public) signposted Semerwater.

The path leads into Semerwater Nature Reserve and offers a spectacular aspect of the water and surrounding hills. Reaching a ladder stile, turn left along the lane towards Semerwater Bridge.

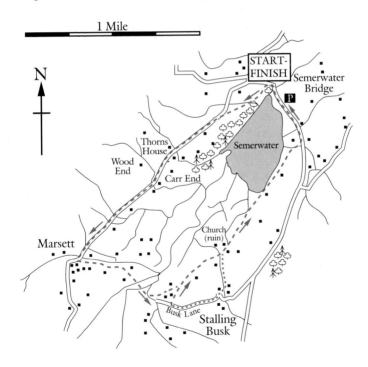

* Note the huge boulders resting at the shoreline of the lake. These are known as The Carlow and The Mermaid stones. Made of limestone, they are thought to have been deposited at this location by glaciers thousands of years ago.

The landscape artist JMW Turner RA incorporated the Carlow Stone in his depiction of Semerwater.

Publisher's Note
The information given in this book has been provided in good faith and is intended only as a general guide. Whilst all reasonable efforts have been made to ensure that details were correct at the time of publication, the author and Dalesman Publishing Company Ltd cannot accept any responsibility for inaccuracies. It is the responsibility of individuals undertaking outdoor activities to approach the activity with caution and, especially if inexperienced, to do so under appropriate supervision. They should also carry the appropriate equipment and maps, be properly clothed and have adequate footwear. The sport described in this book is strenuous and individuals should ensure that they are suitably fit before embarking upon it.